ISBN 978-1-5276-8185-9
PIBN 10880580

1 MONTH OF
FREE
READING

at

www.ForgottenBooks.com

By purchasing this book you are eligible for one month membership to ForgottenBooks.com, giving you unlimited access to our entire collection of over 1,000,000 titles via our web site and mobile apps.

To claim your free month visit:

www.forgottenbooks.com/free880580

English
Français
Deutsche
Italiano
Español
Português

www.forgottenbooks.com

Mythology Photography **Fiction**
Fishing Christianity **Art** Cooking
Essays Buddhism Freemasonry
Medicine **Biology** Music **Ancient**
Egypt Evolution Carpentry Physics
Dance Geology **Mathematics** Fitness
Shakespeare **Folklore** Yoga Marketing
Confidence Immortality Biographies
Poetry **Psychology** Witchcraft
Electronics Chemistry History **Law**
Accounting **Philosophy** Anthropology
Alchemy Drama Quantum Mechanics
Atheism Sexual Health **Ancient History**
Entrepreneurship Languages Sport
Paleontology Needlework Islam
Metaphysics Investment Archaeology
Parenting Statistics Criminology
Motivational

THE POST-MILLENNIAL ADVENT

THE Church has always held the doctrine of the Second Advent. But occasionally, and only occasionally to any considerable extent, has the question of the *time* of the coming agitated the minds of Christians.

At Thessalonica after the reception of Paul's first epistle there was a pre-millennial excitement, which was caused by hasty interpretations of certain passages. On this account and more fully to instruct the erring, the apostle said in his second letter, " Now we beseech you, brethren, touching the coming of our Lord Jesus Christ, and our gathering together unto him ; to the end that ye be not quickly shaken from your mind, nor yet be

5

troubled, either by spirit, or by word, or by letter as from us, as that the day of the Lord is now present; let no man beguile you in any wise."—2 Thess. ii, 1-3.

Again, in the midnight of the Dark Ages, in the year 999, when the lamp of knowledge was well-nigh extinguished, many people imagined that the Saviour was then coming. Indeed, so greatly were some disturbed in mind that in the churches and in the shadow of the churches multitudes slept during the last nights of the tenth century. But this planet and the heavenly bodies went on in their usual courses, and the excitement died away.

Even in the present day there have been premature expectations concerning this great event. In 1843 unwise speculations on this subject disturbed some communities in New England.

6

But the doctrines of Pre-millenarianism are conspicuous by their absence from the great Creeds of Christendom.

In the Apostles' Creed, which had its origin in the days of primitive Christianity, are these statements : "From thence he shall come to judge the quick and the dead ;" "I believe in the resurrection of the body."

The Nicene Creed, which was formulated in 325 A. D., declares : "And he shall come again with glory to judge the quick and the dead;" "I look for the resurrection of the dead and the life of the world to come."

The Athanasian Creed, which is placed in the fifth century, contains the following : "From whence he shall come to judge the quick and the dead. At whose coming all men shall rise

7

that have done
:o life everlast-
at have done
ng fire."
gnificant that
atholic Creeds
lennial claus-
er hand, they
ly favor the
Dr. Wil-
s that Mil-
no means
ith of the
by its ab-
y Creeds."
"the doc-
ıl coming
ed from
eds, the

ranted speci
rousia may I
never disturb
thinkings of]
ity.

Furthermor
these Creeds, t
possesses six
uable docum
that really giv
the faith of t
versal.

The Prayer
palianism is a v
iment of holy
Thirty-nine Art
less a good s
Christian faith
century, and it:

again with their bodies; and shall give account for their own works. And they that have done good shall go into life everlasting, and they that have done evil into everlasting fire."

It is highly significant that these three great Catholic Creeds contain no pre-millennial clauses, while, on the other hand, they do most unmistakably favor the post-millennial view. Dr. William B. Pope affirms that Millenarianism was "by no means at any time the faith of the Church, as is proved by its absence from all the early Creeds." He further states that "the doctrine of a pre-millennial coming of Christ was excluded from every form of early Creeds, the keynote of all these being, FROM THENCE HE SHALL COME TO JUDGE THE QUICK AND THE DEAD." From these facts it is fair to conclude that whatever unwarranted speculations on the *parousia* may have occurred, they never disturbed the theological thinkings of primitive Christianity.

Furthermore, in addition to these Creeds, the Christian world possesses six pre-eminently valuable documents — documents that really give a consensus of the faith of the Church Universal.

The Prayer Book of Episcopalianism is a venerable embodiment of holy teaching. Its Thirty-nine Articles give doubtless a good summary of the Christian faith of the sixteenth century, and its fourth article, on the Resurrection of Christ, affirms : " Christ did truly rise again, and took again his body, . . . wherewith he ascended into heaven, and there sitteth until

9

he return to judge all men at the last day."

There is another very venerable document, the Westminster Confession of Faith of Presbyterianism. In reference to Christ, the Mediator, in chapter eight, article four, it declares: "On the third day he rose from the dead with the same body in which he suffered; with which he also ascended into heaven, and there he sitteth at the right hand of the Father, making intercession; and shall return to judge men and angels at the end of the world."

The Augsburg Confession was drawn up under the supervision of Luther and Melanchthon. The original document was read before Charles V. in 1530. This Confession is the chief standard of faith in the Lutheran Church, and largely represents the Prot-

eaven, and in our
:ontinues, until he
gain to judge the
dead."

Catechism of the
:atholic, Eastern
h is the Greek
:s the same doc-
ng the *parousia*.
was approved by
and received the
Czar of Russia
aff's Creeds of
ɔl. ii, pp. 445,
lly pp. 479—481.
4.)

of Methodism,
:nerable, is a
nfluential doɔ

and its
held in
learning
third arti
tion of Ch.
did truly
dead and
. . . . whe
into heaver
until he ret
at the last d
. Surely it ɪ
the three Cre
Church and
sions of Prot
their doctrina
any bearing
most decidedl
lenarianism.

we find these words in answer to question forty-six: "That Christ was taken up in sight of his disciples into heaven, and in our behalf thus continues, until he shall come again to judge the living and the dead."

The Larger Catechism of the Orthodox, Catholic, Eastern Church, which is the Greek Church, teaches the same doctrine concerning the *parousia*. This Catechism was approved by the Holy Synod and received the sanction of the Czar of Russia in 1859. (Schaff's Creeds of Christendom, vol. ii, pp. 445, 542. See especially pp. 479–481. Questions 226–234.)

The Discipline of Methodism, though not a venerable, is a highly venerated, influential document. It gives both polity and theology to one of the most *spiritual* and intelligent post-reformation, ecclesiastical organizations. Its evangelistic work and its Scriptural teachings are held in honor by the piety and learning of Christendom, and its third article, " Of the Resurrection of Christ," declares: " Christ did truly rise again from the dead and took again his body . . . . wherewith he ascended into heaven, and there sitteth until he return to judge all men at the last day."

Surely it may be asserted that the three Creeds of the primitive Church and the great Confessions of Protestantism, so far as their doctrinal statements have any bearing on the question, most decidedly favor Post-millenarianism. Dr. William B. Pope says that " Mediæval Chiliasm was generally the badge of fanatical and heretical sects," and that " there have been no if Christ has already come, the Church has been in a most grievous error during all these centuries in celebrating the Sacrament of the Lord's Supper. Every minister of the Gospel is very familiar with these words : "For as often as ye eat this bread and drink this wine ye proclaim the Lord's death till he come."—1 Cor. xi, 26. Thus the whole of Christendom has been under a dreadful delusion for nearly two thousand years, or Christ did not come at the destruction of Jerusalem. We may be assured that Whedon is right when he says : "Nor is Christ represented as coming at the destruction of Jerusalem."

In the Apocalypse of Daniel and in that of John a clear light is thrown upon this question of the Second Advent. But it seems expedient at present to

the
riev-
cen-
acra-
pper.
pel is
rds :
this
le ye
h till
Thus
n has
lusion
years,
it the
We
lon is
or is
ing at
m."
Daniel
clear

2. "And as he sat on the Mount of Olives, the disciples came unto him privately, saying, Tell us, when shall these things be? and what shall be the sign of thy coming, and of the end of the world?"—Matt. xxiv, 1-3.

I.

1. "And Jesus answered and said unto them, Take heed that no man lead you astray. For many shall come in my name, saying, I am the Christ; and shall lead many astray."

2. "And ye shall hear of wars and rumors of wars; see that ye be not troubled; for these things must needs come to pass; but the end is not yet."

3. "For nation shall rise against nation, and kingdom against kingdom; and there shall be famines and earthquakes in divers places. But all these things are the beginning of travail."—Matt. xxiv, 4-8.

4. "But take ye heed to yourselves; for they shall deliver you up to councils; and in synagogues shall ye be beaten; and before governors and kings shall ye stand for my sake, for a testimony unto them."—Mark xiii, 9. "Settle it, therefore, in your hearts, not to

meditate beforehand how to answer;
for I will give you a mouth and wisdom,
which all your adversaries will not be
able to withstand or to gainsay."—Luke
xxi, 14, 15. "And then shall many stumble, and shall deliver up one another,
and shall hate one another. And many
false prophets shall arise, and shall lead
many astray. And because iniquity
shall be multiplied, the love of many
shall wax cold. But he that endureth
to the end, the same shall be saved."—
Matt. xxiv, 10-13.

5. "And this Gospel of the kingdom
shall be preached in the whole world
for a testimony unto all the nations;
and then shall the end come."—Matt.
xxiv, 14.

II.

1. " But when ye see Jerusalem com-
passed with armies, then know that her
desolation is at hand. Then let them
that are in Judea flee unto the mountains; and let them that are in the midst
of her depart out : and let not them
that are in the country enter therein.
For these are days of vengeance, that
all things which are written may be
fulfilled."—Luke xxi, 20-22.

coming on the world; for the powers of the heavens shall be shaken. And then shall they see the Son of man coming in a cloud with power and great glory."—Luke xxi, 25-27.

5. "And he shall send forth his angels with a great sound of a trumpet, and they shall gather together his elect from the four winds, from one end of heaven to the other."—Matt. xxiv, 31.

III.

1. " But when these things begin to come to pass, look up, and lift up your heads; because your redemption draweth nigh."—Luke xxi, 28.

2. "And he spake to them a parable: Behold the fig tree, and all the trees: when they now shoot forth, ye see it and know of your own selves that the summer is now nigh. Even so ye also, when ye see these things coming to pass, know ye that the kingdom of God is nigh." Luke xxi, 29-31. " Verily, I say unto you, this generation shall not pass away, till all these things be accomplished. Heaven and earth shall pass away, but my words shall not pass away."—Matt. xxiv, 34, 35.

3. " But of that day and hour know-

eth no one, not even the angels of heaven, neither the Son, but the Father only."—Matt. xxiv, 36.

4. "And as were the days of Noah, so shall be the coming of the Son of man. For as in those days which were before the flood they were eating and drinking, marrying and giving in marriage, until the day that Noah entered into the ark, and they knew not until the flood came and took them all away; so shall be the coming of the Son of man. Then shall two men be in the field: one is taken and one is left; two women shall be grinding at the mill; one is taken, and one is left. Watch therefore: for ye know not on what day your Lord cometh."—Matt. xxiv, 37-42.

5. "But know this, that if the master of the house had known in what watch the thief was coming, . . . There shall be weeping and gnashing of teeth."—Matt. xxiv, 43-51.

IV.

1. "Then shall the kingdom of heaven be likened to ten virgins. . . . Watch therefore, for ye know not the day nor the hour. For it is as when a man,

22

of

he

aro

ll :

tch

hat

civ.

ster

.tch

nall

"—

tven

atch

nor

nan,

the destruction of the templ
This meant a great deal to th
Jew ; and therefore, in his di
course, Jesus often returns 1
the *taula*, the "these things
that refer specially to the temp
and city—to the external ove
throw of Judaism.

2. The disciples have no
been with their Master for thre
years, and must have bee
taught many things concernir
the purposes of God and mu
have known the bearing of the
leading questions about th
" these things," the Second Cor
ing, and the end of the worl
or *æon*. This phrase, "the en
of the world," is used in th
parable of the tares so as to d
fine its meaning. " The harve
is the end of the world. *Æ*
therefore the tares are gathere
up and burned with fire ; s
shall it be in the end of th

24

clore, in his dis-
often returns to
"these things,"
lly to the temple
: external over-
l.

les have now
[aster for three
t have been
gs concerning
od and must '
aring of their
about the
Second Com-
the world,
:, "the end
sed in the
io as to de-
'he harvest
'orld. As
gathered

ol the w(
come forth
from amo
Matt. xiii, 3
be no doub
as intelligen
the vast cont
ing answers
prehended.

1. Jesus beg
a caution agai
This was nec
says that "fals
orned by zea
people in a feve
as though the I
still appear." In
deceived multitud
the city, and on
the

Lord's earnest and repeated warnings caused the Christians to depart when Titus came against the city with his legions, and thus saved the Mother Church of Christendom.

2. Jesus, after speaking of wars and rumors of wars and comforting his disciples, distinctly informs them that "the end is not yet;" or, as Luke expresses it, "the end is not immediately." Some say that Christ here refers to the destruction of Jerusalem. But, taking a general view of this discourse, it would appear that he answers their last question first. In that case the reference is probably to the primitive days of Christianity. Then political commotions were prominent features history; and though there we persecutions, the Church tended and grew mightily, u

and repea
the Christi
Titus ca
ith his legic
the Mot
idom.

speaking
of wars a
isciples, d
m that "t
or, as Lu
end is r
me say th
the d

_ year, this brings us
own through the Dark Ages,
hen millions suffered death for
hrist. Memorable centuries of
iminent peril and dire distress !
mid throes of travail died the
artyrs whose blood was the
ed of the Church ; and with
unutterable pangs the Church
ought forth reformers who
ught the battles of civil and
igious liberty for mankind.
ring these dismal ages God
l a tower of refuge for his
ple in the wilderness of the
ine Mountains. Assuredly,
light was set on a hill for
ination and for safety.
igh Romanism ravaged all

years, yet the dragon was not ab
to devour our blessed Christiai
ity, the child of the Church an
the destined ruler of the nation

4. In this part, as might b
expected, our Lord prepares h
followers for great trials. H
comforts their minds by a speci:
promise that words and wisdoi
will be given them when brougl
before rulers. Then, again, fo
low very sad predictions. Man
shall stumble, false prophei
shall arise, hatred shall show i
self, iniquity shall increase, an
the love of many shall grow col(
But salvation shall be given t
them that are faithful to the en
of life.

5. Now comes the welcom
announcement that the Gosp(
of the kingdom shall be unive
sally preached for a witness (
testimony. There has been di:
cussion on this word " witness.

ot able
istian-
h and
ations.
ht be
es his
. He
pecial
isdom
ought
n, fol-
Many
phets
w it-
, and
cold.
en to
e end

come
ospel
iver-

the peo

re need

his ma

themse

ppy re:

vorld-v

d a vi:

out ha

ed, gr

filled

n plai

gdom

crush

fill t

divin

all-sub

ity an

of the

truth

phant anthem : " The Kingdo
of this world are become t
Kingdoms of our Lord and
his Christ."—Rev. xi, 15.

Trusting in the Holy Gh
one may safely conclude t
the preaching, the witnessing
unto salvation, and that in 1
good time coming the world w
be full of testimony for Chr
and full of believers. T
state of things will surely gi
humanity a thousand joyc
years of a highly Christi
civilization. "And then sh
the end come," according to 1
words of the Great Prophet.
the foregoing paragraphs is 1
divinely given order of ever
and the Second Advent is 1
placed before the general dif
sion of Christianity among 1
nations.

II.

1. Having just given in outline the history of his Church, Jesus begins again at Jerusalem, and more fully explains certain matters, of paramount importance. Urging his followers to make good their escape, he pathetically utters predictions of sorrow and slaughter attending the siege by the Romans.

2. There is here a return to the subject of false Christs, and that his followers may know how to detect them a certain sign is given. The Lord tells them that when he comes it will be with inimitable celestial manifestations. Merely to fully inform his disciples against deceivers, without reference to the chronological order of events, at this place is introduced a description of the *parousia*. It was

needful for the Jerusalem Christians to have this sign in reference to the manner of the coming, that they might be in no danger from deceivers, and in no danger of perishing in the destruction of the city. That such was the purpose in mentioning the *parousia* in this connection is evident from the context. In the very next verse, which must refer to the Roman army, are these words : "Wheresoever the carcass is, there will the eagles be gathered together." Evidently the destruction of Jerusalem, false prophets, and the necessity of enabling his followers to detect deceivers are the great thoughts now in our Lord's mind ; and his reference in this place to the coming is merely explanatory. Thus understood, the passage is quite plain, and does not disturb the order of events.

3. There is foretold in t
part the destruction of the cı
the saddest captivity of ı
Jews, and the fulfilling of ı
times of the Gentiles. But iı
intimated that this, the long
captivity, will have an end.
it not in harmony with the ic
of a universal Christian civili.
tion that wealthy converted Je
should take an interest in ı
Holy Land, and should bu
beautiful homes amid the p
cious memorials of the prophe
priests, and kings? They v
love the sacred places that hc
blessed memories of their lor
rejected, but now lovingly ɛ
cepted, Prince of the House
David. Railways are alrea

Jacob for an everlasting posses
sion. Why should not our *holy*
religion make the world in gen—
eral, and Palestine in particular,
bloom as the rose and flow with
milk and honey ?

But we must return to our
subject and give attention to
the latter part of Luke's statement : "until the times of the
Gentiles be fulfilled." These
words are of such large import
that they must be interpreted
by the Scriptures themselves.
Happily Paul gives us the con-
tent of this passage in Romans,
where he says,

" Now, if their fall is the riches of
the world and their loss the riches of
the Gentiles, how much more their fullness."—Rom. xi, 12.

Again, in verse 25:

" For I would not, brethren, have
you ignorant of this mystery, lest ye be
wise in your own conceits, that a hard-

ent

g posses-
our ho
l in ge
articula
flow wi

n to c
ention
e's sta
s of t
'   The
ge imp
terpret
emselv
the c
Roma

e riches

iour places these times of fu
ness before his Second Advent

4. To aid the student it ma
be suggested that the wicked
ness of the Jews after Pentecos
foreshadowed the little season c
apostasy which will follow th
millennium, according to Rev
xx, 3 ; that the portents whic
Josephus declares appeared i
the heavens prefigured the in
describable concomitants of th
parousia ; and that the destruc
tion of Jerusalem represente
the final catastrophe of th
world. However, it is plain tha
after the fullness of Jews an
Gentiles there will be wonderfu
appearances in the heavens, di:
tress among the nations, an
finally the coming of the Son c
man. This order of event
which is given by Luke is th
same as that given by John i
*Revel*ation. After the miller

nium—sad thought !—part of humanity will relapse into wickedness. Then strange astronomical signs will appear, and fear and apprehension will overtake the backslidden nations. And finally shall be seen the infinitely glorious presence of the Judge Eternal.

5. After the solemn and dreadful declarations of the previous predictions, another comforting and gracious promise is made to the faithful. Amid the universal consternation and confusion their precious dust shall be remembered and shall be gathered from the four winds of the earth.

III.

1. Once more the Saviour comes back to the *tauta*, the "these things," that refer to Jerusalem, and comforts his lis-

is another guiding sign con-
ing the then near future.
is, moreover, tells them
nly that " these things," the
a of their first question
ch referred to Jerusalem and
city, are nigh at hand—that
is generation shall not pass
y till all *these things* be ac-
plished." That generation
witness the establishment of
Kingdom of God on the day
Pentecost, the overthrow of
aism, and the destruction of
and temple. Note that the
a is in the first question and
no reference to the Second
ent.

Jesus further teaches men
the times are in God's
ping, and that men especially
t be contented with only a
ly outlined knowledge of the
it future.

. The suddenness of the

43

foreign country—into a "far country," according to the Authorized Version. This fact should prevent any from placing undue stress upon such words as *immediately*.

2. We now approach the closing part of this glorious Apocalypse; and reverently would we listen to the awful sentences that are so easily understood. Here the Divine Majesty speaks in sublimest and simplest language, and settles the question under discussion. The Saviour finally and plainly states to his disciples that when he comes in all his glory, with the holy angels, there will be the general judgment of all nations, and the appointment of all human beings to their final states. These most solemn declarations closing the Apocalypse unmistakably show that the Second Advent and the Judgment

of *all* mankind will take place at one and the same time.

Thus this prophetic discourse, beginning with Jerusalem and ending with the consummation of all things, when its parts are placed in their order, outlines in simple language the history of the Church, and proves that Christ will not come until after the millennium—until the last day; until the end of the world; until the general judgment. Notwithstanding this, the bride through all the centuries longingly and lovingly looks forward to the appearance of the bridegroom. Also, often in her loneliness and afflictions has she exclaimed, " Come, Lord Jesus !" But the bride must wait in patience, must attend to the duties of the hour, and must guard against false announcements and false bridegrooms.

It is apparent that the Great Prophet in this wonderful Apocalypse gives a simple and straight answer to our question. He has arranged the leading events of Church history in their true order, and has placed his coming after the millennium. Our question is really answered. Still, it may be well to show that the general trend of Scripture is in harmony with this Apocalypse and to explain certain misunderstood passages.

In accordance with the foregoing post-millennial conclusions are the plain eschatological declarations of Scripture.

Hear Daniel: "And many of them that sleep in the dust shall awake, some to everlasting life, and some to shame and everlasting contempt."—Dan. xii, 2. The prophet evidently believed that there will be only *one* resurrection, and that it will take place at the time of the general judgment.

Listen to the Saviour : " Marvel not at this: for the hour cometh in which all that are in the tombs shall hear his voice, and shall come forth : they that have done good unto the resurrection of life; and they that have done evil unto the resurrection of judgment."—John v, 28, 29. Can there be any reason for not understanding this emphatic statement? The Saviour is very definite: " The *hour* cometh in which *all* the dead," the good and the bad, "shall come forth." It is impossible to explain away such passages. They are unanswerable proofs that there will be but *one* resurrection previous to the one judgment.

Mark Paul's declaration can before Felix and the assembled Jews and Gentiles: "There shall be a resurrection of the dead, both of the just and of the unjust."—Acts xxiv, 15. In similar language the Apostle warned the Athenians: "He hath appointed a day in the which he will judge the world in righteousness."—Acts 17, 31. These are noteworthy expressions—*a* resurrection for both the just and unjust ; *a day* for judging the world.

Observe Peter's explicit prediction: " The day of the Lord will come as a thief in the night; in the which the heavens shall pass away with a great noise, and the elements shall melt with fervent heat, the earth also and the works that are therein shall be burned up."—2 Pet. iii, 10. This clearly shows that " the day of the Lord," which is the *pa-*

From the foregoing quotations it must be inferred that Daniel, our blessed Lord, Paul, Peter, and John believed in post-millenarianism. We are, therefore, warranted in concluding that the whole drift of Scripture favors the synchronizing of these four eschatological events; namely, the *parousia*, the resurrection, the end of the world, and the judgment of the whole human race.

1. There will be only one resurrection.

2. It will take place at the Second Coming.

3. The Second Coming will be at the end of the world.

4. At the end of the world will be the general judgment.

These conclusions cannot be set aside, because they are clearly and repeatedly revealed in Holy Writ. Even if two or three

51

rump; for the trumpet shall
ound and the dead will be
ised incorruptible."—I Cor. xv,
, 52. These verses present
difficulty. In truth, they
or Post-millenarianism.
ut the next passage for con-
ration has caused a good
of trouble, and one should
oach it in a reverent and
rful spirit. In Second Thes-
ians Paul instructs his err-
rethren and tells them not
beguiled—tells them of
nan of sin," "the son of
n," that will sit "in the
of God, setting himself
God." Now comes the
ifficult the

is doubtless correct. "In many respects," he says, "the Pope has an indisputable claim to these titles. He is emphatically the man of sin." Of late some have been giving a pitiably insignificant explanation by calling Nero "the man of sin"—Nero, who was merely one of the despicable emperors of Rome. But Romanism, the vile mother of unutterable monsters and unparalleled crimes which darkened long ages into blackest night—Romanism, "mystery of iniquity," somewhat adequately corresponds to the stupendous and appalling metaphors of Scripture. The old commentators knew this antichrist better than we do, and were assured that only the diabolism of Romanism could answer this description of the "son of perdition."

Now, Paul states that this

"man of sin," this antichrist of
all the antichrists, will have his
period before the *parousia*. This
is generally believed. And, if
Romanism is tottering to the
fall, which appears to be the
case, may not the Second Advent be expected at any mo-
ment? In answer, observe, the
apostle states that by " the
breath of his mouth" Christ
shall slay this "man of sin."
The Authorized Version reads:
"The spirit of the mouth."
But this breath or spirit of
his mouth can mean nothing
else than the preaching of the
Gospel in the power of the
Spirit. According to Isaiah:
" He shall smite the earth with
the rod of his mouth, and with
the breath of his lips shall he
slay the wicked."—Isa. xi, 4.
It is plain, therefore, that by
preaching, which is the two-

edged sword that proceeds out of the mouth of the Lord, "the man of sin" will be slain. Yes, Christianity will destroy the papacy. This prediction accords with the signs of the times. What vast triumphs have been won since the days of Luther! In no country can the Inquisition now burn a Christian, and only in the very darkest parts of the earth can priests burn Bibles. Indeed, at the present time under the very walls of the Vatican the Holy Scriptures are sold. Moreover, public sentiment is so generally Christianized that the Pope is beginning to talk patronizingly of the Word of God. The temporal power has gone, the influence of the priesthood is going, and the mother of abominations is becoming such a noisomeness in the nostrils of nations that soon

llennial Advent

and outraged

ll slay " this m

crisy.

icult passage nee

ation. What is a

e next clause—

ght by the mar

oming ? " De

ng is very e

ilate by the a

oming." Af

ere a difficu

ists ? Is R

royed br

..cn, having the key of the
and a great chain in his
And he laid hold on the
n, the old serpent, which
 Devil and Satan, and
l him for a thousand years
ast him into the abyss, and
it, and sealed it over him
ne should deceive the n
no more, until the the
ears should be finished
nis he must be loosed i
ime.

I saw thrones, and they
upon them, and judg
given unto them : and
souls of them that h
aded for the testimor

Chri
rest
the
finish
recti
that
recti
deat
shall
Chri
a th
"
are f
out
forth
whic
the
gath

1. What sort of persons will be those raised-up saints and those raised-up sinners?

2. What intercourse will the glorified saints have with these resurrected sinners?

3. How does Satan deceive the nations?

(*a*) If they are glorified saints how can he deceive them?

(*b*) If they are raised-up sinners why need he deceive them?

It must be confessed that the literal interpretation of this passage presents manifold difficulties, and really violates both human reason and Scripture usage. In this Book of Revelation especially does one expect to find glorious truth veiled in mystic metaphor. In no other literature of earth are found such elaborate symbols and such stupendous figures of speech. Why attempt to literalize this

..ow naturally these dec-
itions disclose their divine
aning to a spiritual interpre-
on. Call this first resurrec-
i the happy change which
d works in man when he
ies him from a death of sin
a life of righteousness. Is
the preacher orthodox when
proclaims : " Awake, thou
sleepest, and arise from the
l, and Christ shall give thee
? " The whole host of the
ch Militant has already
ed from death unto life."
!lievers must yield them-
"unto God as those that
ie from the dead." The
ig father said truly "T

On a certain occasion Pope Adrian used this language: "The heretics Huss and Jerome are alive again in the person of Martin Luther." A similar use of speech is found in the case of Elijah, concerning whom Malachi made a prediction: "Behold, I will send you Elijah the prophet before the great and terrible day of the Lord come." —Mal. iv, 5. Jesus explained this when in speaking of John the Baptist he said, "This is Elijah which is to come." These are not orientalisms, but common figures of speech.

Here, then, is the explanation of this much-misunderstood passage. The martyrs and confessors will live again in their godly successors, and in the doctrines for which they suffered. The glorious company of the reformers, like their ascended

the glory of God. Of the coming splendors of the Church wise Solomon caught a glimpse and uttered his welcome. "Who is this that looketh forth as the morning, fair as the moon, clear as the sun, and terrible as an army with banners?"—Song vi, 10.

Summing up the foregoing, it may safely be concluded that the great coming events of human history will be in the following order:

1. The millennium, a period of divine blessing and material prosperity, brought about by the present ministries of the Holy Ghost through the preaching of the Gospel.

2. The little season of apostasy when Satan shall be allowed for a short time to deceive men.

3. The Second Advent of our Lord in indescribable glory.

rent

of all th

e work

by fir

ment c

of hap-

fullnes
nk tha
nswere
ch m
ning
eason'
low th

stly e
to b
y pr
work

s
o
w

are infected with Pre-millenarianism. But the believers in
this doctrine are doing very little to save the world. And this
is natural ; for who would wish
to be a witness against men and
to represent a dying cause?

At present our chief duty is
not to indulge in fanciful expectations about the *parousia ;*
but to obey our Lord's com-
mand, "Occupy till I come."
— Luke xix, 13. Let our
motto be like that of the
Salvation Army, "The World
for God," and let our faith
be as large as the Abra-
hamic covenant and embrace
" all families." How the de-
ceiver tries to circumscribe the
promises ! He would fain limit
the Lord's predictions to the
Roman Empire, or to the world
as known by the Apostles. Emphatically repudiate all such

CPSIA information can be obtained
at www.ICGtesting.com
Printed in the USA
BVHW081351210119
538277BV00021B/1166/P